How the Insects Got Their Colors?

"Coloured Bedtime StoryBook"

ILLUSTRATED & PUBLISHED
BY
E-KİTAP PROJESİ & CHEAPEST BOOKS

www.cheapestboooks.com

 www.facebook.com/EKitapProjesi

ISBN: 978-625-6308-92-3

Copyright, 2024 by e-Kitap Projesi

Istanbul

Categories: Animals Arts, Music, Family & Friendship
Country of Origin: Laos
Cover: © Cheapest Books
License: CC-BY-4.0

For full terms of use and attribution, http://creativecommons.org/licenses/by/4.0/

About the Book

When a group of insect friends visit a colorful flower garden, they decide to be colorful too. Which colors will they choose?

How the Insects Got Their Colors?

Pum Anh

"I am yellow," the bee says.

"I mix the red and the yellow," the rhinoceros beetle says.

"That makes orange. Now I am orange."

"I mix the blue and the yellow," the grasshopper says.
"That makes green. Now I am green."

"I mix the red and the blue," the butterfly says.

"That makes purple. Now I am purple."

"I am red," the dragonfly says.

"I am blue," the cicada says.

"I want to be colorful like my friends," the caterpillar says.

"It is not hard at all," the bee says.

"We will help."

"Hooray! We all have beautiful colors."

"Oh! I am seven colors," the caterpillar says.

"Oh! There are many flowers!" the butterfly says.

"Let us be colorful like them."

"Let us go to the flower garden, friends," the butterfly says.

End of the Story